A Crabtree Branches Book

TOP HORSE BREEDS

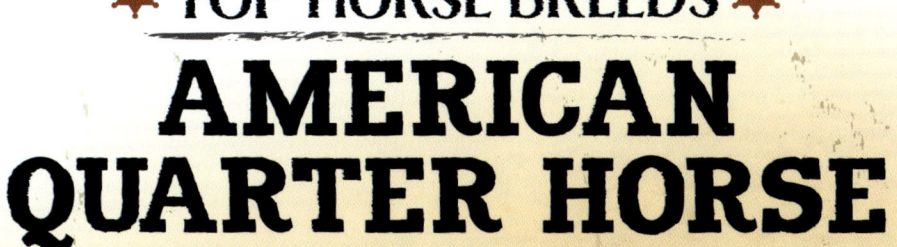

AMERICAN QUARTER HORSE

Kerri Mazzarella

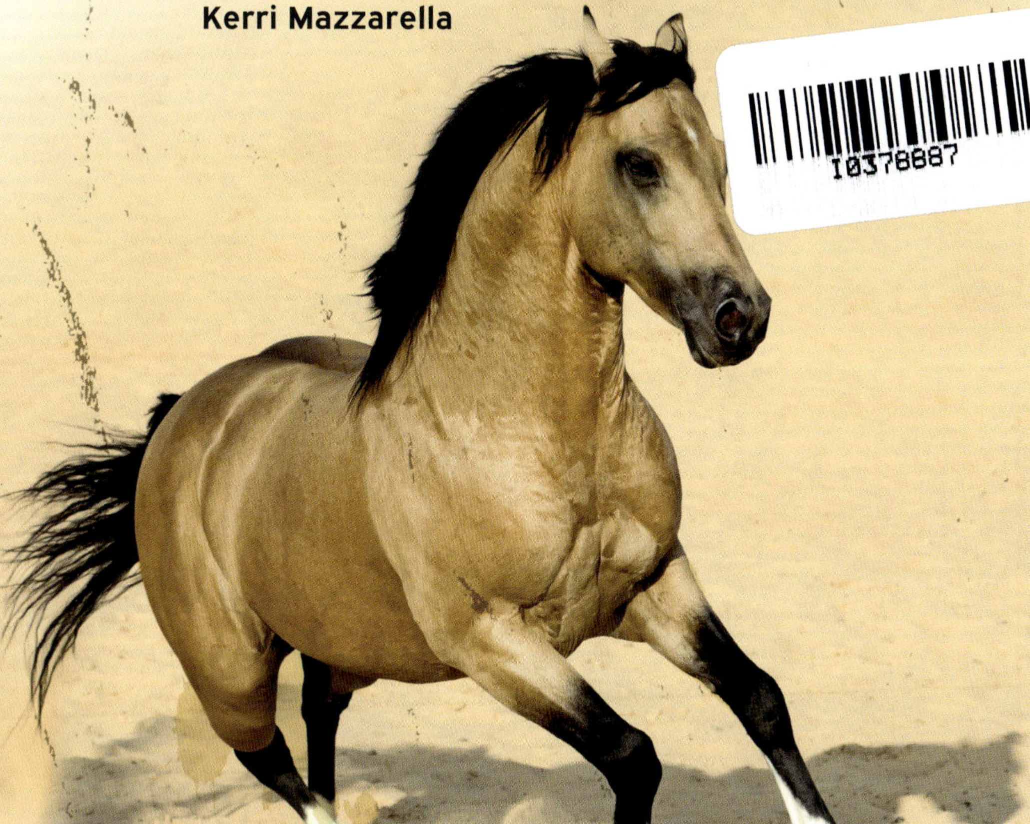

Crabtree Publishing
crabtreebooks.com

School-to-Home Support for Caregivers and Teachers

This high-interest book is designed to motivate striving students with engaging topics while building fluency, vocabulary, and an interest in reading. Here are a few questions and activities to help the reader build upon his or her comprehension skills.

Before Reading:
- What do I think this book is about?
- What do I know about this topic?
- What do I want to learn about this topic?
- Why am I reading this book?

During Reading:
- I wonder why...
- I'm curious to know...
- How is this like something I already know?
- What have I learned so far?

After Reading:
- What was the author trying to teach me?
- What are some details?
- How did the photographs and captions help me understand more?
- Read the book again and look for the vocabulary words.
- What questions do I still have?

Extension Activities:
- What was your favorite part of the book? Write a paragraph on it.
- Draw a picture of your favorite thing you learned from the book.

TABLE OF CONTENTS

History 4

Characteristics 8

Size and Color 12

Care and Feeding 16

Uses, Jobs, and Equipment 20

Cost 24

The G.O.A.T.s 28

Glossary 30

Index 31

Websites to Visit 31

About the Author 32

HISTORY

The American Quarter Horse is a special **breed** that has been around since the seventeenth century. It is the first horse breed **native** to the United States.

In the 1600s, Spanish and English horses were **crossed** with Chickasaw and Mustang horses to create the American Quarter Horse. These horses became known for their friendly personality and fast speed.

In the 1940s, the American Quarter Horse Association (AQHA) was formed to keep a **registry** of the breed. It is now the largest horse breed registry in the world.

DID YOU KNOW?

Wimpy was the very first registered American Quarter Horse. He was born in 1937 in Kingsville, Texas.

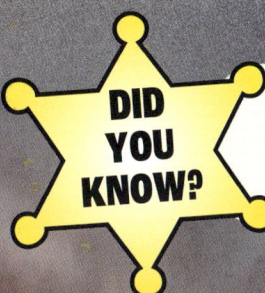

DID YOU KNOW? More than 6 million American Quarter Horses have been registered by the AQHA.

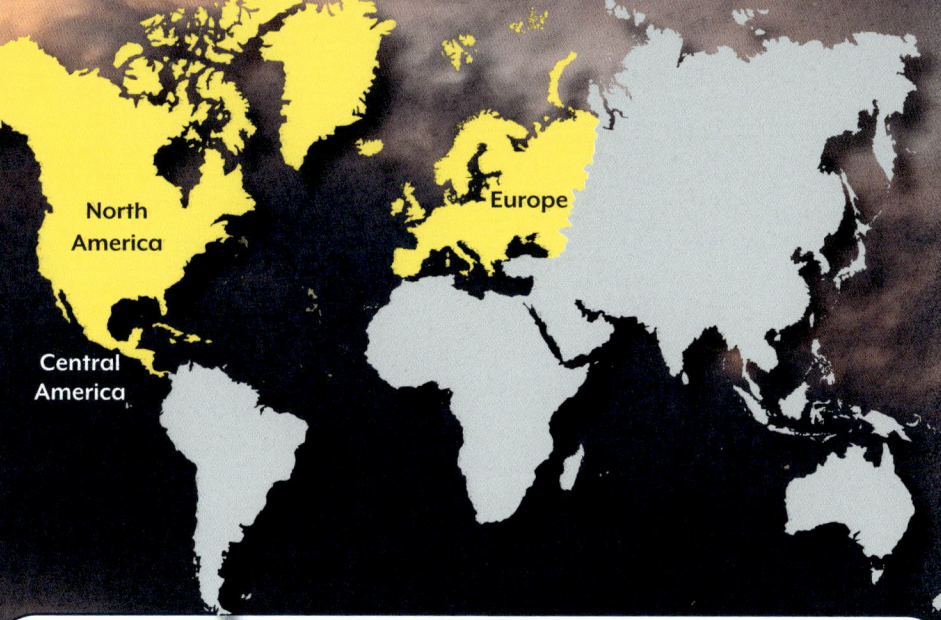

The American Quarter Horse is the oldest and most popular horse breed in the U.S. They can be found in North America, Central America, and Europe.

CHARACTERISTICS

The American Quarter Horse is short, with a muscular build. It is a very fast horse!

DID YOU KNOW? American Quarter Horses got their name from their ability to outrun other horse breeds in quarter-mile races. They can sprint at speeds of up to 55 miles per hour (88.5 km/h).

Quarter Horses have broad chests and very strong back legs. Their powerful legs help them run fast.

The American Quarter Horse has a short, wide head, strong jaw, and small ears. It has excellent balance, hearing, and eyesight.

Quarter Horses are not easily startled. Loud noises and sudden movements do not cause them to **buck** or get upset. This makes them a good horse for beginning riders. They are great with other animals and children.

SIZE AND COLOR

DID YOU KNOW? One hand equals 4 inches (10.2 cm). A horse's height is measured from the ground to the top of its shoulders.

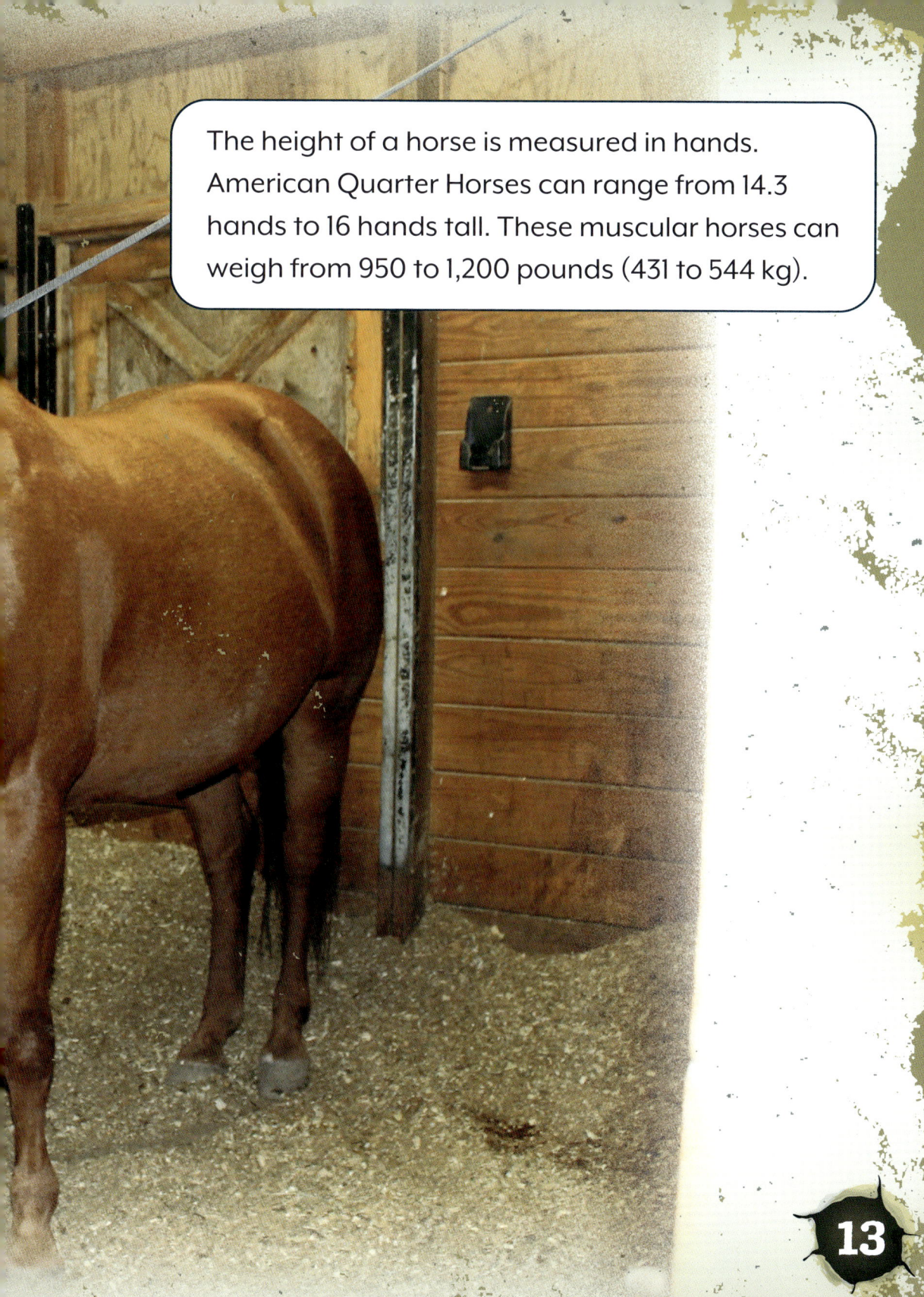

The height of a horse is measured in hands. American Quarter Horses can range from 14.3 hands to 16 hands tall. These muscular horses can weigh from 950 to 1,200 pounds (431 to 544 kg).

American Quarter Horses have short hair and long **manes**. The color of their mane is normally lighter than their hair.

DID YOU KNOW?

There are 17 recognized American Quarter Horse colors: white, grullo, bay roan, buckskin, chestnut, black, sorrel, gray, palomino, bay, cremello, dun, perlino, red dun, blue roan, red roan, and brown.

The most common color for an American Quarter Horse is sorrel, a reddish-brown color.

CARE AND FEEDING

Like all horses, American Quarter Horses require daily care and attention. They need proper nutrition, yearly veterinary visits, and regular **grooming** to live happy, healthy lives.

Exercise is important to keep a horse strong and healthy. An American Quarter Horse should be taken for a ride at least three to five times each week.

DID YOU KNOW? An American Quarter Horse can eat up to 10 pounds (4.5 kg) of grass or hay and drink up to 12 gallons (45 L) of water each day.

American Quarter Horses eat a variety of hay, grass, grains, fruits, and vegetables. They have small stomachs and eat small amounts throughout the day. Horses need lots of clean water to drink daily.

Quarter Horses need to live in an environment that has a shelter for protection from storms and harsh sunlight. They also need a big pasture to **graze**.

DID YOU KNOW? Horses can sleep standing up. And they cannot burp!

USES, JOBS, AND EQUIPMENT

American Quarter Horses are valuable to people all over the world. They can help with jobs on a farm, such as plowing fields, pulling heavy carts, and **herding** cattle.

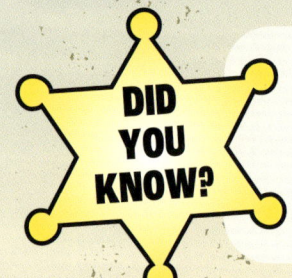

DID YOU KNOW?

The American Quarter Horse has a "cow sense." They have a natural ability to round up cattle.

Quarter Horses are used for many different activities, including **rodeo** events and trail rides. Some are even used as therapy horses.

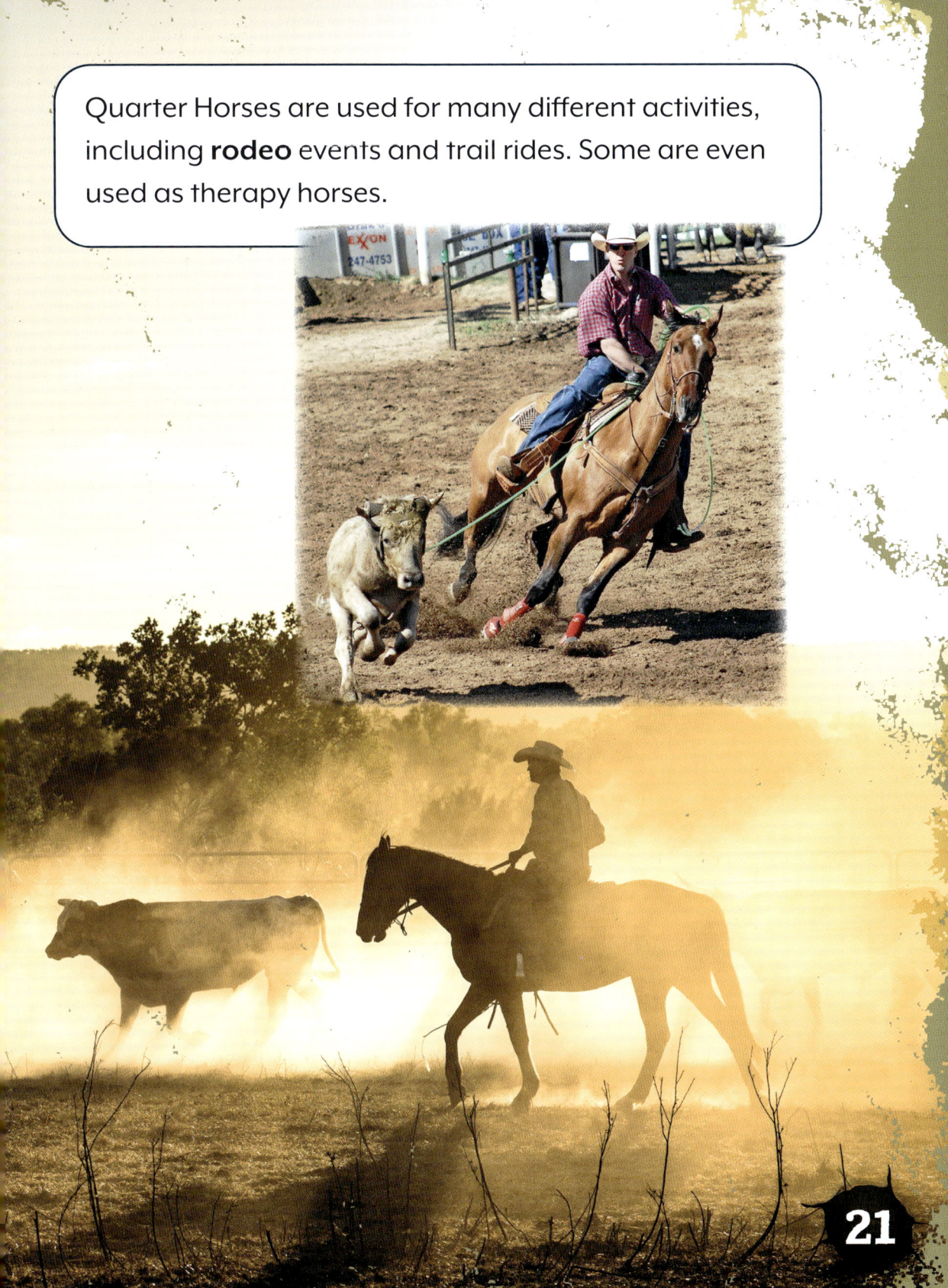

The equipment needed for riding a horse is called horse tack. A saddle should be used for horseback riding. Two popular kinds of saddles are Western and English.

Western saddle

English saddle

Safety is important when riding a horse. They are large, powerful animals that could cause serious injury if not handled properly. Always wear a helmet while horseback riding.

COST

stallion

The average lifespan of an American Quarter Horse is 25 to 35 years. This friendly, strong horse can range in average price from $3,500 to $20,000.

The price of a Quarter Horse is determined by many different things, such as age, **bloodline**, and training. Male horses from a strong bloodline can cost up to $100,000!

mare

foal

DID YOU KNOW? Male horses are called stallions, female horses are called mares, and baby horses are called foals.

Owning a horse can be expensive. The average yearly cost to take care of a horse can range from around $4,000 to $10,000. Housing is the greatest expense and can cost an average of $6,000 a year.

Yearly costs to feed a horse are around $1,000 to $2,000. Veterinary care is usually around $750 a year. Other expenses include grooming products, horse hoof maintenance, and riding equipment.

THE G.O.A.T.s

There are many famous American Quarter Horse bloodlines. The greatest of all time for racing is a Quarter Horse named First Down Dash. He lived from 1984 to 2010. He was **inducted** into the American Quarter Horse Hall of Fame in 2011.

The greatest Quarter Horse of all time for rodeo events is Driftwood. He lived from 1932 to 1960. Driftwood was inducted into the American Quarter Horse Hall of Fame in 2006.

DID YOU KNOW? Driftwood's original name was Speedy.

GLOSSARY

bloodline (BLUHD-lahyn): The ancestors of an animal

breed (BREED): A particular type of animal

buck (BUHK): To jump into the air with the back arched

cross (KROSS): To mix two breeds of animal together to produce a new breed

graze (GRAYZ): To feed on growing grass

grooming (GROOM-ing): The practice of brushing and cleaning the coat of a horse, dog, or other animal

herd (HURD): To move animals as a group

induct (in-DUHKT): To officially make someone or something a member of a special group

mane (MAYN): The long, thick hair on the head and neck of a horse

native (NAY-tiv): An animal or plant that lives or grows naturally in a certain place

registry (REJ-uh-stree): A system for keeping an official list of something

rodeo (RO-dee-oh): A sport where people compete in events such as riding horses and roping cattle

INDEX

American Quarter Horse
        Association (AQHA) 6, 7

breed 4, 5, 6, 7

children 11

color 14–15

cost 24–25, 26–27

hay 18

height 12–13

saddle 22

shelter 19

speed 5, 8, 9, 28

water 18

weight 13

WEBSITES TO VISIT

https://www.aqha.com/educational-resources-activities

https://thesprucepets.com/american-quarter-horse-5272310

https://www.britannica.com/animal/American-Quarter-Horse

ABOUT THE AUTHOR

Kerri Mazzarella lives in South Florida with her husband, four children, and two dogs. She loves horses and has always wanted to own one. Her daughter has taken horseback riding lessons for many years. She hopes you enjoy learning about different breeds of horses as much as she does!

Written by: Kerri Mazzarella
Designed by: Kathy Walsh
Series Development: James Earley
Proofreader: Melissa Boyce
Educational Consultant: Marie Lemke M.Ed.

Photographs: Shutterstock Cover & Title pg: Jaco Wiid, benchart; Background and Border: benchart; p 4: Alla-V; p 5: Rob Palmer Photography; p 7: Semisatch, Puwadol Jaturawutthichai; p 8 Alla-V; p 9: Jaco Wiid; p 10: Jaco Wiid; p 11-12 Merry Barrieres; p 14, 15 Jana Mackova; p 16: LightField Studios; p 18 SchubPhoto; p 19: Luce Morin; p 20: Janelle Lugge; p 21 Warren Price; p 22 Marie Charouzova, Glushchenko Nataliia; p 23: Merry Barrieres; p 24: Lenkadan; p 25: Kwadrat; p 26: Merry Barrieres; p 27: Pixel-Shot, Annabell Gsoedl; p 28: manzrussali

Crabtree Publishing

crabtreebooks.com   800-387-7650
Copyright © 2024 Crabtree Publishing

All rights reserved. No part of this publication may be reproduced, stored in a retrieval system or be transmitted in any form or by any means, electronic, mechanical, photocopying, recording, or otherwise, without the prior written permission of Crabtree Publishing.

Printed in the U.S.A./072023/CG20230214

Published in Canada
Crabtree Publishing
616 Welland Ave.
St. Catharines, Ontario
L2M 5V6

Published in the United States
Crabtree Publishing
347 Fifth Ave
Suite 1402-145
New York, NY 10016

Library and Archives Canada Cataloguing in Publication
Available at Library and Archives Canada

Library of Congress Cataloging-in-Publication Data
Available at the Library of Congress

Hardcover: 978-1-0398-0939-0
Paperback: 978-1-0398-0992-5
Ebook (pdf): 978-1-0398-1098-3
Epub: 978-1-0398-1045-7